ONE DAY WITH GOD

MORE WILDSIDE CLASSICS

ONE DAY WITH GOD

A Guide to Retreats and the Contemplative Life

Revised Edition

by
Bishop Karl Prüter

WILDSIDE PRESS

Copyright © 1991 by Karl Prüter

ONE DAY WITH GOD

This edition published in 2006 by Wildside Press, LLC.
www.wildsidepress.com

CONTENTS

DEDICATION

*To those who have attended the many
retreats I have led over the years.
Thanks for your patience and support.*

Retreat

A place of seclusion, especially
for religious contemplation

INTRODUCTION

Dear Reader:

We would all like to go to a special place of seclusion to spend one day with God. But often we cannot go because of time and financial considerations.

However, with a little planning, we can use our home as our special place of seclusion. I would like also to be able to come to your home and lead the retreat for you. But that, too, is not possible because of time and financial considerations.

This book is my way of being with you when you spend a day in your home with no other guest than God.

I pray that this book will help make your one day with God all you want it to be.

—Bishop Karl Prüter,
Highlandville, Mo
September, 1991

I.

THE CALL TO RETREAT

Approximately ninety-five percent of all people claim to believe in God. Very few claim to know Him intimately. Still fewer ever claim to have heard Him speak and almost none claim to have seen Him. In fact, among those who claim to have seen Him, more than half of them would be judged insane by any competent psychologist. Of course, not all the people who claim to believe in God profess any desire to know Him or even to know more about Him. In short, they can take Him or leave Him. Yet, in America today, one half of the population belongs to a church, meeting, synagogue, or temple. Presumably, these people desire to know God and to serve Him. Yet, here too, we must ask, "How intimately do they know Him and how many have heard His voice or beheld Him with their eyes?" Jesus said truly, "You have eyes and do not see and you have ears and you do not hear." Is He suggesting that mere mortals can hear and see God? Yes, of course, and down through the ages, those whom the church has labeled as saints and mystics, have done so. How, and in what form, I shall discuss later, but for now, let me state that if we do less, our lives are improperly centered and we have closed our eyes and ears to the very God in whom we profess to believe.

The theologians tell us that God is everywhere and can be found everywhere, but they do not tell us why His presence is hidden from all but a chosen few. Further, this lack of awareness of God has never been greater than in our own time. Although Man's material life is greatly improved, and in many parts of the world it is no longer necessary to work from sunrise to sunset in order to provide

11

sufficient food for one's needs—therefore providing more leisure time, the time Man spends in his search for God has not increased. In fact, it is obvious that the time devoted to God and to the spiritual world has decreased.

The Industrial Revolution, which began in the latter part of the eighteenth century, not only changed man's use of his time, but also his ideas of what and who are important. Today, in a survey done in Germany, it was discovered that half of the population believes that religion is obsolete. I suspect another survey would show that almost ninety percent of the same population would say that they believe in God. It is just that He is no longer relevant. The change is obvious in so many areas of our lives. In few homes is Bible reading a daily family ritual. It was before the Industrial Revolution, and that is not so very long ago. Grace at meals is no longer a practice in the majority of homes. Even the Sabbath Day for Jews and Sunday for Christians are no longer scrupulously set aside for the worship of God. Only about twenty-five percent of the American population bother to attend public worship at least once a week. What happened to the twenty hours per week that Americans gained when the work week was reduced from an average of sixty to forty hours? Perhaps if this had happened in the twelfth century, men would have regarded the change as a blessing from God and would have felt that a large portion of the time should be used in His service.

But with the shorter work day came a host of new distractions. The Industrial Revolution brought with it gadgets to use up our time and to fill our world with sounds that not only drown out the voice of God, but also destroy the silence which is the proper environment for the nuturing of Man's soul. Think about your own life. Take just one day of the week. If your home is typical, you get up in the morning feeling harried and hurried. You must wash, dress, have breakfast, and, if you have children, get them ready for school. Somehow, in all this hurry and confusion, you turn on the radio or television to get the morning news. There doesn't seem to be enough confusion and chaos in the home, so you let in the world's share of confusion and chaos to add to that already existing, and in addition, raise the noise level. We seem, in our time, to be afraid of silence. For, if we get into our cars to go to work, we are apt to immediately turn on the radio instead of enjoying a time of relative quiet.

For eight hours, we labor and give our attention to our supervisors and our work. In none of this time do we have time for God. Even the clergyman is so busy in the day to day operations of the parish church, that he ignores the God he is trying to serve. I have talked with "busy" clergymen who complain that they do not have time for devotions. I have spoken with others who have told me that their devotional time is that time when they prepare their Sunday sermon. One is tempted to ask, "How dare they consider writing a sermon before they have spent many hours in intimate communion with God? Should not the sermon grow out of one's relationship with God?"

The argument is often advanced that the best prayer is one's service to God and to one's fellow Man. It is something like the husband who never finds time to talk with his wife, but answers her complaint by saying it must be obvious that he loves her because of all he does for her. Jesus warned us that "not everyone who says, 'Lord, Lord,' shall enter the kingdom of heaven: but he who does the will of the Father." Simply because one decides that he is doing the Lord's work does not always mean that this is what God intends one to do. We must walk with Him in close fellowship if we desire to know what He wills us to do. Further, although God wants our service, He wants our love and our fellowship even more.

When I was a child, my father once instructed me to mow the lawn while he was at work. I forgot his instructions, but during the day, I had this feeling that there was something I was supposed to do for him. I remembered that he had observed that the cellar needed to be cleaned and so I spent several hours carrying out the trash and sweeping the cellar clean. When my father returned home, I told him about my work with great pride and glee, as I was expecting to be praised for my effort. Instead, my father was angry because he had instructed me to mow the lawn. The work that I had done was not "his work." What was important was that I did what he expected of me. How like so many Christians I was: doing things to please that are not asked of them, and neglecting that which they are asked to do. Unfortunately, what we claim we are doing is the "will of God," but we seldom consult Him.

We need to take time out every day to pray and to meditate and to be silent long enough for God to make His will known to us. Sometimes we have a lot of catching up to do and God needs us to set aside an entire day so that He may speak to us of many things. On this "one day with God," we need to come together with our brethren and in silence, each one of us, spend the day in fellowship with God. If you believe in a personal God who desires your love, fellowship, and service you will want to spend many a day with Him in the course of a year. There is no particular way in which the day must be spent, but there must be sufficient silence provided if you are to hear what He wishes to say to you. If the idea of "one day with God" is novel to you and you feel ill at ease about it, read what follows, as there are some ideas so that your day with God may enable you to know Him better, and know yourself better, so that you may come away knowing His will for you.

II.

SHOULD YOU GO ON A *SILENT* RETREAT?

If you have never been on a silent retreat, you may wonder if this is something for you. A whole day of silence sounds threatening, since each day is precious and you want to be certain that this will not be a wasted day. If this has occurred to you, let me offer a word of warning: there is an introduction to the book *The Cloud of Unknowing* that warns the reader about attempting to read the book. The same caution applies equally to participating in a silent retreat, so I shall share it with you. It says:

> Whoever you are who possess this book in any way—whether you own it, or have borrowed it, or simply carry it for another—I charge you by a vow of love that you will not willfully read it, nor write it, nor speak it, nor even permit it to be read, written or spoken by anyone else, nor to any other person, except by one whose purpose, in your judgment, is to become a perfect follower of Christ. By that I do not mean a person who is devoted only to deeds of mercy, but one whose purpose is to come to the pure contemplation of God, or to the most sovereign point that is possible for him to come to in this temporal life. He should be one who does all he can to help himself on in this life by a faithful heeding of moral and spiritual disciplines and has been doing so for a long time.
>
> By this same vow of love I charge you

that if any such do read it, write it, or speak if, or hear it read or spoken, that you will charge them as I do you, to take time to read, write, speak or hear the whole book; for there are some matters in the beginning or middle part that are left hanging, and yet are taken up later, and if a man saw only one part and not the other, he might easily be led into error. That you and others may avoid this error, I charge you to do as I tell you for love's sake.

As for worldly chatterers, self-praisers and blamers, tale-bearers, gossipers, and all kinds of fault-finders, I do not care if they ever see this book. It is not my intention to write such a book for them, and it is better that they do not meddle with this one. I would say the same also to all curiosity seekers, whether they be learned or unlearned. It may be that they are good men in their daily lives, but a work on contemplative prayer could mean little to them. This is not true of those who remain outwardly active in the world but are nevertheless drawn to a life of contemplation through an inner longing for God, whose own Spirit calls them, and whose laws are beyond their present comprehension. These men are not continually aware of this inclination of their souls (as is the case of true contemplatives) but now and then they do partake of a true oneness with God. If such men were to see these words, they would be greatly strengthened by them through the grace of God.

If you should attend a silent retreat, it is possible you will learn things about yourself that may cause you pain and dismay. Many years ago, I attended Calvary Episcopal Church in New York City one evening in July. Before I entered the church, I met a young man who was going to the Vesper Service for the first time. At that time, Calvary Church had a very excellent choir and many people attended primarily to hear it. That night, I thought, they sang unusually well and I felt the music would lift me from the pew. After the service, as we were descending the steps, he turned to me and said, "Wasn't that hell?" He had been bored to tears and his remark left me shocked and confused. Upon further reflection, I realized that many people do not enjoy good music, beautiful sunsets, or great art—they are bored to tears.

A day of silence will undoubtedly not thrill everyone. Yet, I urge everyone to try it, contrary to the advice the author of *The Cloud of Unknowing* shared with would-be readers. Regardless of how you react, you will learn something of great importance. Either the day will prove to be a truly high point in your life, never to be forgotten, or it will be a long, tedious, and boring day. If it is the latter, think for a moment of what it would mean.

If your thoughts were on God, and they brought you no pleasure, what does this say about you? If you find no pleasure in the presence of God, you are truly lost to Him. Somewhere or somehow you taken a wrong turn and missed the meaning of your creation and your life. Perhaps, you plead, it was only that you did not sense God's presence during the day of silence. But why not?

In the Holy Scriptures we read that Jesus was disappointed when He asked His disciples to stand watch while He was in prayer and they fell asleep. He asked them, "Could you not watch one hour with Me?" If your daily prayers are extremely short, it may be due to the pressure of the daily routine, or it may be that you are bored with God. When you go on a silent retreat it may be a moment of truth. Surely, it is not too much to ask that once in a while you spend a day with Him, who created you, sustains you, and provides you with all that you have. If you cannot give Him one day, what joy will you find in spending Eternity with Him?

A silent retreat provides the best conditions under which we can open our hearts and minds to His presence. It doesn't guarantee that His presence will excite us. Many will find themselves in this condition and many more will find themselves unable to even consider spending an entire day with God. They are simply not thrilled at the prospect of spending one day with Him. If this is your situation and you are concerned about it, I would suggest a time of preparation. In the following chapter, I shall offer some ideas that may enable you to spend one day with God and come away knowing that you have been in His presence and be refreshed in mind, body, and soul, and inspired to serve Him. May I also recommend to you the following prayer by Thomas à Kempis:

> Give me, O God, that spirit of interior recollection which will make me attentive to Thy holy will and faithful to Thy graces. Grant that the remembrance of Thine awful presence may remind me continually of blessed life and conversation, and effectually control me during my earthly pilgrimage. I am weary, O God, of living in exile from Thy presence, and of being so little affected by the consideration of Thy majesty as to do nothing to please Thee. What can I find in heaven or on earth that is comparable to Thee? Thou are the God of my heart; grant I may be ever sensible of Thy presence, and desire only the happiness of pleasing Thee in time, that Thou mayest be my portion for eternity. Amen.

Give this prayer some thought and if you want to feel as did Kempis, you may want to go on a retreat. But this book is written for those of you who cannot go away to some distant retreat place. Your one day with God can be spent at home—by setting the day aside. You need to take the phone off the hook, send the children to your parents, and resolve to not answer the door. Then find a quiet place in the house and speak only with God. You may wish to read the following selections to help direct your thoughts toward Him. I have suggested that you may want to spend

18

some time in meditation between each selection, but these times are totally arbitrary. Do not turn away from God in order to read, but rather read in order to turn your heart and mind toward Him. Go now to your closet and there spend the day in peace and quiet with the One who gave you life and breath and who promises to guide, instruct, and preserve you unto Life Eternal.

III.

THE MOUNTAIN

There lived in a small Syrian town two men, one a Christian and one an atheist. For years the atheist had observed the Christian and envied his peace of mind and his composure at all times.

At last, convinced that the Christian God might be real, he approached the Christian and asked whether it would be possible for him to obtain from God this peace of mind which he had observed in the Christian.

The Christian replied, "Yes," if he would get acquainted with God. The atheist said he would be willing to try, but just where could he meet this God?

The Christian told him that it was his custom to go out beyond the village about three miles and there on the road in the country, he would meet and converse with God.

The atheist went out the next morning and after he had gone three miles, he came before a mountain. He stood before the mountain and shouted loudly, "Lord, God, make known unto me what kind of being you are!" When he received no response, he shouted again and again, "Lord, God, make known unto me what kind of being you are!" But, alas, his efforts were in vain.

Still he came back the next day and the next day for nearly a month, and then disgustedly he concluded that he had always been right—there was no God.

Sometime later, he again saw the Christian and he tauntingly remarked that he had gone out to meet God but He was not to be found and that the Christian's peace of mind and sense of well-being was nothing but self-deception.

"Did you go out from the village three miles as I di-

21

rected you?" asked the Christian.

"I did, and then I stood before the mountain and shouted unto your God."

"There is no mountain there," replied the Christian, "but no matter. What did you say unto the Lord?"

"I said unto Him, "Lord, God, make known unto me what kind of being you are.""

"Ah," replied the Christian, "when I go out there, I shout unto the Lord what kind of being *I* am. I confess unto Him that I am sinful and cannot exist pure and holy apart from Him. Then He appears unto me and I can better understand what kind of being He is."

The next morning the atheist went out, and fell on his knees before the mountain and said, "Lord, I am a sinful man, forgive me and make me clean."

The mountain vanished and he knew that it was only a shadow of his own self, and when self no longer stood between him and God, he saw the Lord.

IV.

A POSTSCRIPT TO THE MOUNTAIN

The message of the story is clear. God is discernible to all who wish to see Him. We are only prevented when our sins cast a shadowy mountain between ourselves and God. A selfish act, an impure thought, an unresolved resentment, become mountains blocking our view of the Lord.

During this day, we shall, each of us, in silence, surrender to God whatever fault within us that would block our view of God. "The pure in heart shall see God," simply means that if we come to Him in innocence, He will not hide Himself from us. As we come before Him in silence, let us ask Him to forgive our sins and save us from wanderings of mind, and strip us of all that would cast a mountain between Him and us.

Finally, Christ has promised that if we have faith, we can remove mountains. In faith then, let us use the silence of this day to be with God, now, tomorrow, and forever!

Recommended time of silence

20 minutes

V.

SEARCHING FOR GOD

One of the exciting things about our times is the number of people who are searching for God. Believe me, in my lifetime I have not seen so many people searching for God in so many ways. One of the frightening things of our times is the ignorance in which many of these people have attempted their search. There are three very prevalent fallacies or pitfalls which many in this generation fall into.

First, the idea persists that you can use God. I heard on the radio an announcement by a scientology teacher, that went like this: "There is a higher force and you can make it work for you." There *is* a Higher Force, who desires that I work for Him. God is not to be used. He seeks to use us in the building of His Kingdom. And if we seek Him to use Him, He will elude us, for such would be contrary to His purpose for us. His love and concern for us demands that we come to Him as obedient and willing servants.

A second fallacy that has been around since the beginning of time, is the notion that our search for God is one of life's little extras—a bonus, so to speak. So many look at God as someone who will be the capstone of a successful life. The final prize at the end of a long series of victories. But God is not an extra. He must be central in our lives. He comes before our careers, our families, and our security. God will settle for nothing less than a total commitment. He will choose your career, your spouse, and he demands that you put your trust in nothing or anyone but Him. "Seek ye first," Christ said, "the Kingdom of Heaven, and all the rest shall be added unto you."

And finally, what does Jesus mean when He tells us

to "Pray without ceasing"? He meant to save us from the third great fallacy: the notion that God will come whenever we beckon or call. The gulf between God and us is almost always very wide. We can only span it by constant prayer. I find that whenever I let down and neglect my devotions, I have moved away from God, and it takes much effort and unceasing prayer to find my way back. If God seems far away from you, which one of you, do you suppose, has moved? God is constant, eternal, and always present. But all this is brought to naught by our neglect and our preoccupation with other things. By it, we have removed ourselves from God.

If you wish to serve Him, you must be constant in prayer and unflagging in your devotions. Then He will give to you out of His abundance, and direct you in His way, and be your constant and close companion, and you shall have life abundant and Life Eternal.

Recommended time of silence

20 minutes

VI.

MEDITATION ON THE MEANING OF THE PHRASE, "SERVANT OF GOD"

"Happy that servant who is found at his task
when his master comes!"

—*Luke* 12:43

Jesus often compares our relationship to God to the master-servant analogy. It simplifies so much. If we would govern ourselves as servants, we would know from day to day what God expects of us. A servant knows the tasks that his master has given him to do. He has only to do them faithfully, thoroughly, and with care. And when he finishes his task, he does not stand around idle, but finds other tasks to do until his master comes and gives him new orders.

A good servant never says, "But I have been given no assignment." When his master returns, he must drop what he is doing and listen to his master's instructions.

A good servant does not grumble at his assignment, nor treat it as his special preserve which he may keep forever. He stands ready to follow his master wherever he goes and easily gives up one task to take up another.

Finally, it is his master and not the servant who determines whether what is being done has worth. For if it is his master's work, then the value of that work has already been determined. What is important in the mind and the heart of the master, must be important to the servant also.

God has given us many tasks, but He has taken unto Himself the cares. We need never worry whether anything has value, or whether it is a success or failure, or even if it

27

will ever be completed. For God has taken all these cares unto Himself. Ours is the simple task of doing God's work each day, seeking no reward except to serve Him faithfully.

Recommended time of silence

15 minutes

VII.

SILENCE

Before all else, there was silence! Silence is primeval and is as necessary to man's well-being as water, food, and shelter. Too often we think of silence as the absence of sound, but we should regard sound as the absence of silence. In the world of the twentieth century, silence is hard to find. Sadly, many do not wish to find it and find themselves uncomfortable in silence.

If you live a typical American life, you break the silence of the morning with the sounds of an electric shaver or electric toothbrush. When you come to the breakfast table, you turn on the radio or television, partially for the morning news or for music, but you also want to drive away the silence. When you get in your car to go to work, you again turn on a radio, even though it may repeat the news you have just heard and the same commercials, *ad nauseam*. The work place is noisy, as are the streets and the markets. There is no escape even in the elevators or the washrooms, as Muzak is designed to save you from silence. If you make a phone call and are put on hold, the welcome silence will be broken by music of someone else's choosing. It is hard to find a quiet place to have lunch or dinner. One, of course, could escape by going walking, jogging, or running, but then why do I see so many with headphones? There is something about silence that we have come to fear. In fact, it has become the tool of police and terrorist interrogation. It is not the questioning that the victim has come to fear, but rather the silent pauses. Early in my ministry, I inadvertently discovered that when I made pastoral calls, many people felt conversation had to be a continuous, uninterrupted round of talking, and that nothing was so intimidating as silence. It was tempting to say, "I think you should help out the parish by becoming a Sunday school teacher," and then pause. If you give arguments, you lose, but silence can win the day. Salesmen, politicians, and interrogators use it and perhaps have tarnished the good name of silence. On the other side of the coin, lovers walking through the countryside know how silence alone can bring two hearts closer together. Artists seeing a beautiful scene for the first time want silence, as if the eyes could not function as well if there were sound. Strangely enough, the loud, tumultous music of Wagner becomes most moving when the last clanging note is followed by silence. Sometimes, although rarely, the applauders are restrained for a few seconds, before fouling the silence that follows with their clapping.

Silence is not just the absence of sound, but it is something basic to our being. It fills a need for the healthy and it can bring comfort and healing to the sick. Far more potent that David's harp, silence is a potent tool of healing. Unfortunately, modern hospitals choose to ignore this, and instead bring to the patient's bedside phones, radios, and television sets. And while it may seem more like home, these things add nothing to the healthy atmosphere of either the hospital or the home.

Wordsworth said, "The world is too much with us," but perhaps it is the world's sounds that are too much with us. The human body, mind, and soul, crave silence, and it behooves us to overcome our fear of it and satisfy this longing of the human soul. If we accept the premise that beauty is necessary for a full life, then we must seek out silence, for silence has a beauty of its own and enhances the beauty that we see in nature. If you have ever sat on a mountain top and surveyed the country below, you must realize that what you saw was even more beautiful because of the awesome silence which surrounded you. Art galleries maintain a quiet because curators realize that a painting viewed in the midst of noise is less beautiful than when it is contemplated in the midst of silence. One really cannot appreciate the great art treasures housed in museums on days when noisy crowds gather around every object to be viewed. If you feel the need to go on a guided tour, promise yourself that you will return someday to view the sculpture, the paintings, undiminished by the drone of the guide's voice. The beauty of art will show itself in greater force in the midst of silence. Not only does silence enhance the beauty of art, but adds to the experience its own sublime beauty.

This being so, should not our visits with God take place not only in the beauty of holiness, but also in the beauty of silence? There is a time to shout His praise and to sing His glory, but there is also a time to be silent. The psalmist has said, "Be still and know that I am God." How often have we told our children or subordinates to be quiet, for I can only hear one of you at a time? If we come into God's presence, it is not likely that we will hear Him if we have given our ears to others who are about us. Even the preacher who pronounces the Word of God from the pulpit, may be doing us a disservice by drowning out the personal words of direction which God wishes to say to us without an intermediary. A church service which makes no provision for silence is incomplete. At the Mass, when Christ is most intimately present, we need a moment of silence so that He may speak to our needs.

Silence is not only beautiful, but it is also God's opportunity to speak to us and be heard. It is an opportunity we sometimes consciously, but most often unconsciously, deny Him. We often treat God as we do a small child. When the child impatiently strives to give an urgent message, we admonish him by saying, "Why didn't you tell us this before?" His plaintive reply is, "I tried, but everyone was talking and I didn't get a chance." If God wanted to speak to you about something important, is there a time in your busy day when He would get a chance? A time when neither employer, customer, family member, friend, casual acquaintance, radio or television voice do not have your primary attention? Even the devotional book you may read (including this one) may serve to shut out the God whom you profess to seek.

God is everywhere and can be found everywhere, but will He find you? The writer of the 139th Psalm says with confidence, "Whither shall I go from Thy Spirit? Or whither shall I flee from Thy presence? If I ascend up into heaven, Thou art there; if I make my bed in hell, behold, Thou are there. If I take the wings of the morning, and dwell in the uttermost parts of the sea; even there shall Thy hand lead me, and Thy right hand shall hold me. If I say, "Surely the darkness shall cover me," even the night shall be light about me. Yea, the darkness hideth not from Thee, but the night shineth as the day; the darkness and the light are both alike to Thee." But the psalmist does not say that the noise and silence are alike to God. God must often feel like a stranger at a party at which the other members chatter on about matters which interest only them and from which he is excluded. Nowhere does it say in the Scriptures that Man cannot exclude God from his life. It is not enough to say, "Speak to me, O Lord, for Thy servant heareth." We must maintain silence long enough to hear.

Recommended time of silence

20 minutes

VIII.

THE GOD WHO SPEAKS

There are many reasons why we enjoy silence, but the quintessential reason is that it affords us an opportunity to hear the voice of God. "Be still and know that I am God" is the greatest lesson of the psalmists. Although God can be heard over the sound and the tumult of the world, we are more likely to hear His voice when we enjoy the peace and serenity of the natural world. Further, God, for all His power and might, cannot speak to the vast majority of men and women because they permit the world's tumult to drown out the voice of God in their lives.

The Quakers refer to the still, small voice within. It is a good description, for seemingly it cannot be heard by those who are filled with earthly sound and fury. God does speak to us, but we are easily distracted. Even more frequently, we are so insistent upon what we have to say to God that we listen poorly to Him, or not at all. During your "one day with God" make use of the silence. Enjoy it for its own sake, but, more importantly, look upon it as an opportunity to converse with God.

Yet keep in mind that God speaks to us in many ways. There are even times when God seems to shout in order to command our attention. I remember many years ago visiting a Maine trapper who had been ill for over four weeks. I expected to find him depressed and despondent, for he loved the out-of-doors, and confinement had to be difficult for him. Instead, I found him cheerful, even radiant. He told me that he had used the time in bed to try to understand his situation. He said, "I honestly feel that God permitted this illness to happen because I needed to do some thinking." What concerned him was his lifestyle. As

33

a trapper and a guide, he was away from his home and family too much. He was having a ball, but it was hard on his family. In part, they missed him very much when he was away, but they also could barely survive on what he was able to earn. In the past, he had been a dairyman and a good one. Now, as a result of his prayers and meditation while he was ill, he felt that God wanted him to return to dairy farming and give up trapping and guiding. My friend acted on what he believed was direct guidance from the Holy Spirit and the events that followed transformed his personal and family life.

I have known others who used their times of trouble to listen and were convinced that God, unable to get their attention any other way in good times, permitted trouble to overtake them so that He could be heard. But it need not always be that way. In a copy of *Reader's Digest* (August 1977), I ran across this story.

> During my early August visit to Petersburg, Alaska, where the annual precipitation is nearly 110 inches, the unexpected happened. More than a week of sunshine blessed the community. It was not until I went shopping one afternoon that I realized the weather was more than a subject for idle conversation. Some stores had "closed" signs in their windows. The one I liked best said: "Owing to an act of God, we are closed today. He sent this beautiful weather, and we believe He meant for us to fishing."

Well, why not? God speaks to us in mysterious ways. For some, through tragedy, but for others, and perhaps those more sensitive to His voice, through beauty and through joy.

Allow me to suggest to you several ways in which God speaks. First, through the Scriptures. Most of our guidance and our direction from God comes from this source. Jesus, through his life, has shown us what is good and how he expects us to live. While these rules are general, they cover most of the ethical decisions we shall ever have to make.

God also speaks specifically to us. He is our Creator and His work in us is never finished. Evelyn Underhill says, "The moment in which, in one way or another, we become aware of this creative action of God and are therefore able to respond or resist, is the moment in which our spiritual life begins."

God speaks to us in a personal way through the events in our lives. Through experience, we come to recognize this subtle way in which God addresses us. Couples who have lived together for many years are familiar with this kind of speech. Although no words may have passed between them, one partner recognizes the needs and the desires of the other. The unuttered language is unique to every couple. I am convinced that God also approaches each of us in a similarly unique manner. Thus, we make a mistake when we read the lives of the saints and try to follow too closely in their footsteps. God's way with each of us is always unique. St. Ignatius of Loyola was converted when he saw the leaves of a tree budding out in spring. He was so moved by this evidence of the wonder and glory of God, that he was led to consider his own place in the world. He found it wanting and changed his way of life. The Apostle Paul encountered Christ on the road to Damascus. Many years ago, I met a traveler who wanted to go to Damascus in the hopes that she, like Paul, would meet Christ there. But even as Paul did not expect to find Christ there, your road, your place of meeting, could be anywhere or at any time. I do not know whether the traveler I met ever went to Damascus, but I assured her that each one of us can expect his or her own Damascus-like road experience without ever leaving home.

Christ's most important gift to us is His presence at Holy Communion. He came into our lives and promised never to leave us. While he is always near to us, His full and bodily presence at the Holy Eucharist provides us with an opportunity for communication that meets our every need. Of course, mere attendance at Mass is insufficient. Whether you will communicate with Him at Mass depends on you. Assuming that you make a good confession at the beginning of the Mass and leave behind any hatreds, resentments, selfish desires, and dishonest thoughts, He will make Himself evident to you. Christ has promised that "the pure in heart shall see God." It is a condition and promise, and His promise He will surely keep.

To experience the presence of Christ at the Mass, we must expect Him, and we must open our hearts to Him. God seeks to enter hearts which await Him, desire Him, and have prepared for Him. One condition of that preparation is that we are ready to serve God. It is this last which is so difficult to do. For God speaks to those who are willing to carry out his commands, for unless we are willing, it would be useless for God to speak. When we are engaged in His work, we hear clearly the things He has to say to us. His work does not drown out His voice. It is only when we serve ourselves and the world that we raise such a tumult that His voice is unheard. We need to approach God daily as did the prophet Samuel and say, "Speak, Lord, for Thy servant heareth."

Recommended time of silence

30 minutes

IX.

WHAT DOES GOD REQUIRE OF THEE?

"What does God require of us?" To live according to His commandments, certainly, but even more. We are working with Him here on Earth for the building of His Kingdom. It means we must work for this end under the direction of the Holy Spirit. Not only must we allow the Holy Spirit to select our vocation, but every detail of our job must be done according to His will and direction. No detail is too minute and none is beneath His concern. Whenever we make decisions, we must not decide alone, but we must submit to His will and directives. The saints were distinguished not simply by their goodness, but because they were good people *led by God*. They knew that it was not sufficient to let God help us decide between right and wrong, for such choices are easy. But God wants to help us choose between equally good choices. For it is not enough that the choice be moral, for unless God desires that particular choice for us, it is not the right choice. For God has a plan for each of us. In His plan for us, He has provided more good things for us than we can imagine, and He desires to lift us to heights which we often have regarded as impossible dreams.

To know God's will is not all that difficult. If you would know a person's will, human or divine, you must be close to that person. And so, through prayer, meditation, and the study of God's Holy Word, we strive to be close to Him. We strive also to seek those things that He loves. We try to be just, kind, and generous to our fellow man. But above all, we seek His Heavenly Kingdom. As we pray, "Thy Kingdom come," we remind ourselves that this world is not our home and that our allegiance is to no state, but to God's Kingdom. To be a member, we need to do but one thing: to obey His Holy Spirit in every act, whether sacred or secular. For when we do His will, we walk with Christ toward one Father with one mind. Although it sounds almost too simple, we need to realize that we can only walk with Christ when we avoid the many distractions of the world in which we currently exist. Anything that takes our hearts and minds away from God, we call sin. Sin is simply the separation of man from God. When we quarrel with our fellow man, we no longer walk with Christ, and we no longer see clearly the will of God. Men lose sight of God, not because He moves away from them, but because they move away from Him. Other times we lose sight of Him because we have allowed envy and strife to come between us. We have often used the phrase that a person was "blind with rage." But we probably have never realized that rage can make us so blind that we can no longer see God clearly. So also can selfishness, envy, lust, dishonesty, and lying, and for this reason God has forbidden these things. For they not only cause harm to our fellow men, but they take away our sight and we no longer see the spiritual world, and we no longer can see God.

For Jesus has promised us that "the pure in heart shall see God." Once we are in tune with God's Holy Spirit, all things will be clear, and we shall see God and the Kingdom in which He dwells.

Recommended time of silence

20 minutes

X.

UNCEASING PRAYER

"But when ye pray, use not vain repetitions
as the heathens do, for they think that they
shall be heard for their much speaking. Be
not ye therefore like unto them, for your
Father knoweth what things ye have need of,
before ye ask him."

—*Matthew* 6:7

One day, I offered to pray for the particular need of
someone who had come to me for counsel. I was asked not
to: never mind the reason, for that is not the point. What
is of interest is the discussion we had concerning prayer and
the pastor's role. I was asked if I would offer prayer for
this person's need even if he did not want me too. My reply was, "No, not if you don't want me to." Later, when I
thought about it, I realized my answer not only did not
make sense, but it was a promise that I could not possibly
fulfill.

Let us think about the situation. A person has
shared a particular need with me. I am concerned and I
sincerely desire that our Father in heaven will give him the
help he needs to resolve this problem. Jesus tells us that
my love for this person and my concern for his need *is* my
unuttered prayer. Even while I was promising not to pray,
God was hearing the prayer of my heart. Anyone who
loves God and knows that He is listening to our hearts, can
no more stop praying than he can stop breathing, or have
thoughts, or feelings. God hears, and that is prayer in the
fullest sense of the word.

Once we put our trust in God and resolve to center

39

our lives around Him, our thoughts and our feelings become our life in prayer. Verbal prayers are more of a way of expressing our need to praise God and to tell Him of our love for Him. For He knows our needs and He cares about us. And when we come to accept this truth in our lives, we look only to Him and our lives truly become unceasing prayers.

Recommended time of silence

20 minutes

(You may want to break the time into two parts to enable you to read this chapter a second time.)

XI.

FOR WHOM SHOULD WE PRAY?

Everywhere the Scriptures tell us to pray constantly, but it is surprising how little we know about this activity. One of the most persistent questions that arises is "For whom should we pray?"

First of all, let me say that you ought to pray for yourself and for your own needs. There are many people who question whether or not they should do this, because it seems so selfish. Someone once told me that nowhere in the Bible are we instructed to pray for ourselves. I said it wasn't true because Christ instructed us to pray for our enemies and, obviously, we are often our own worst enemies. I was not trying to be facetious, for unless a man learns to love himself he will be a problem to others. Further, Jesus taught us the Lord's Prayer in which we pray for our daily bread and for the forgiveness of our sins.

The world is too full of people who want to solve everyone else's problems before they have solved their own. We need to be reminded of the fact that the world is all right; it is only the people that make it bad. I know of no other way to make the world better than to change the people in it, beginning with myself. Unfortunately, many people want to make the world better by starting with the other fellow. Yet by all means pray for your own needs. God knows them, and He is aware of how much they occupy your time and efforts, and unless we unburden ourselves to Him, He cannot show us how to effectively dispose of our problems. God wants to help us with our burdens and bids us to come to him with our troubles.

If we want further scriptural justification for going to Him with our personal concerns, we have the example of Jesus, who asked God to spare Him the bitter cup, if possible, but, in any event, was willing to submit unto the will of the Father.

Next, we probably should pray for the enemies outside of ourselves, for it is this group of people who most often frustrate us. Christ told us to love them, yet often they are the most unlovable. Since it goes against our nature to love them, we need God's help. And God does help. Sometimes He shows us where we are at fault, and thus we see the need to change. Sometimes He shows us how we can help bring about a change in our enemies. Usually, if we can show our enemies love, something does happen, and they and we become different. At least our relationship becomes better. There are times when our love cannot penetrate, but God's love can and often does. The reason so few of our enemies seem never to change for the better is that we pray for them so seldomly. We simply lack faith that God can change human nature and thus, year after year, human nature remains the same. Those Christians who knew Saul when he was breathing threats against them must have felt that all the prayer in the world would avail nothing. Yet Saul, the persecutor of the Christians, could not remain the same when Christ chose to intervene. So when Christians pray for their enemies, more often than not they will see great changes in the lives of those for whom they pray.

We need to pray daily that we may never wish ill to our enemies nor bend our knees before insolent might. We need to resist evil with good, and to ask God's blessing upon all whom we encounter. Of course, we should do as much for our friends as for our enemies. We often take our friends for granted and it is a pity. Just because their friendship comes without asking is no reason to neglect them in our prayers. What are their needs, their hopes, their concerns, and their problems? Often you know the answers better than do your friends, and you ought to do something, but what? To speak of these needs to your friends may often injure the friendship, but you can speak to your friend's friend, the Almighty God. Time and time again, I have known tremendous miracles to take place, all because someone cared enough to pray. There are times when God wants you to speak to your friend regarding his needs, but often He would prefer that you be quiet and let Him do the speaking. In the meantime pray, and if God wants anything further from you He will find a way of letting you know.

Finally, we need to pray for all those for whom we have a special concern. As Christians we most always address God on behalf of the whole church. Usually we say "we" rather that "I," for we are not alone in our concerns and our petitions. So we daily pray for the whole church that God might grant the church His special blessing.

Who occupies a special place of concern in your heart? If it is a departed loved one, speak to God about this person. We know so little of the future life that unless we unburden ourselves to God, we feel a concern that this is unnecessary. Further, except for God we have no fellowship with those saints who are departed, yet through Him we are bound together in one perfect and eternal body: the Church of Jesus Christ.

So great were the prayers of Jesus on behalf of the dead that some were restored to life. Perhaps this is not within our power, but, by Jesus' own example, we are justified in voicing our innermost concerns and desires to God. For God has promised to heed our every request and has set no limit either on what to pray for or for whom we may pray. He has asked us to pray without ceasing—even for those who hate and despise us—and He has promised that He will turn no man away with a stone, but as a loving Father he will feed us all with the bread of life.

Recommended time of silence

20 minutes

XII.

MAKING THIS DAY COUNT

"Take no thought for tomorrow, for tomorrow shall take thought for things of itself. Sufficient unto the day is the evil thereof."
—*Matthew* 6:34

Nowhere is Jesus more down to earth and practical then when He advises us to live one day at a time. For by attending to today's affairs, we make the future stable and predictable. The man who sows today will reap tomorrow, and in life's normal rhythm few things will take him unawares. The surprising thing about life is how few are the big surprises that we encounter. It is fortunate, too, because the human soul seems to be able to stand little that is unexpected or uncertain.

During the Great Depression an incident occurred that initially delighted the country. A man who made his living walking through the city carrying two boards advertising a diner one day found a bundle of securities in the gutter. He returned to the owner nearly $90,000 worth of securities and, in turn, the owner rewarded him generously with $5,000 and a job as a messenger for the brokerage firm. Four months later, the country was saddened to hear that his unexpected good fortune seemed to have completely deranged the man, and he had to be confined to a mental hospital. Whether our surprises are good or bad, we seem ill equipped to handle them. Fortunately, few of us have to endure more than three or four real tragedies in our lifetimes. But the loss of a home through fire, or the early death of a parent or child through an accident, take their

45

toll, and often require months of adjustment.

But we are hardly much more prepared for the good things. We may not be like the sandwich board man, but nevertheless, it is a rare individual who can handle unexpected and unearned good fortune. A number of years back, a group of Amish left their farm lands when oil was discovered in the area because they did not wish to accept something they had not earned. Others might talk of good luck or bad luck, but what they sowed today, they would surely reap on the morrow. The Amish preferred to live one day at a time, trusting in God to make the future bright.

Oddly enough, many people regard Jesus's sermon on trusting God to provide for them as impractical. They insist they are not like the birds of the air and that God helps only those who help themselves. Let us not misread what Jesus told us. We are expected to help ourselves and this is precisely why Jesus places the emphasis upon today. You cannot do much about tomorrow, but today is yours to use and to plan. What Jesus is saying is that if you use today wisely, tomorrow will take care of itself.

I remember talking to a thirty-five-year-old telegrapher who felt that his life was shattered because the railroad for which he worked was phasing out telegraphers. He, along with thousands of others, was engaged in a long strike to force the railroad to continue to employ unneeded telegraphers. After all, he pointed out, he had given fifteen years of his life to this occupation and it would be difficult at this age to train for something else. The tragedy was that for the entire fifteen years, he knew he was working in an obsolete trade, but did nothing about it. The second tragedy was that he still could not live for the day, but was rooted in the past. Of course, a thirty-five-year-old man *can* train for another job or profession. This man's problem was that he simply could not live one day at a time.

Anyone who has set out on a long journey or a long training or re-training program can tell you that you cannot worry about how long it is going to take. You live each day for itself and tomorrow has a way of coming, usually without incident or surprises. Most of our surprises are not

46

surprises at all, and most of our tragedies need not be. The young aspiring executive who comes home with the glad news of a promotion really surprises no one. He has lived each day for itself and those who knew him best knew that promotion would come—they just did not know *when*.

A friend of mine illustrates the other side of the coin. He found himself financially embarrassed and explained the cause was an unexpected expenditure to fix a leaking roof at his parent's house. None of it squared with reality. He was young, unmarried, and had held a good job for several years. Had he lived each day well, he would have had something set aside for the inevitable rainy days. One wonders about the parents also, who put off providing day by day for the inevitable roof repairs of tomorrow. The tomorrows very soon become today.

It is not Jesus, but we who are often impractical. We often worry about tomorrow rather than do the things that need doing today. Setting aside something today is more practical than worrying. Most of us regard ourselves as practical, and yet whatever befalls us, we so often find ourselves victimized by the things that we neglected to do yesterday. Take no thought for tomorrow for the very practical reason that today's tasks are all that any of us can handle, and for the delightful reason that if we attend to today's needs, tomorrow has a way of taking care of itself.

This is Christ's way of bringing order to chaos and enabling us to live peaceably with a full measure of security in Him.

Recommended time of silence

20 minutes

47

XIII.

THE GREATEST THRILL

We eagerly seek to meet politicians, presidents, kings, queens, and Hollywood and television stars. We not only seek to meet them, but at times we are satisfied just to catch a glimpse of them as they ride by in a stretch limousine. Few, however, experience a similar thrill at spending a few moments with God. A few saints have felt the thrill and the excitement that others accord to movie stars, but very few others. Perhaps that is why they are called saints. If you have a moment which you could take from your busy day to go to a quiet church, or some secluded spot in the country and there meet with God, how excited at the prospect are you? Does the opportunity of meeting with Christ at the Mass produce a thrill compared to that of meeting some Hollywood celebrity? Or let's suggest another analogy. When you were courting, remember how you felt when you left your work place and hurried to meet your loved one? This is, in a smaller way, the thrill we ought to feel when we find a few moments to be with God. If we do not feel something like this, we must ask "Why?"

For some of us, God has never seemed as *real* as those we see in the flesh. More likely, if we are less than thrilled about being with God, it is because we do not share the same interests. The goal of the saint or mystic is to merge his will with God's so that he has no will than that which God wills, and takes pleasure only in those things which please God. For we are never more excited than when we are in the presence and in the company of those with whom we share all things in common. When our wills are one with God's we become thrilled by His presence. When His joys are our joys, we take delight in His presence. There is no better measure of our spirituality than the joy we feel when we are alone with God.

Recommended time of silence

20 minutes

XIV.

THE LONELINESS OF GOD

We all, at sometime, experience loneliness. Some people, because they have few opportunities to be with people, feel lonely; yet others feel especially lonely because they are surrounded by people but have no meaningful relationship with anyone. Old, childless couples may miss having children, but others, because their children ignore them. Imagine, then, God's situation. He has countless children and the vast majority have never spoken a word to Him. A large number never say His name, except to curse Him. Surely one of the reasons, if not *the* reason, why God created Man is that He was lonely in the vast universe that was His. All people, even the Deity, desire to communicate with others.

Of course, we cannot force others to communicate with us. But, by being a friend of all, some will seek our company. If none do, we should remember that God does. The answer to our loneliness is to seek the fellowship of God. We should offer our friendship to alleviate His loneliness and, by so doing, we shall find the answer to our own. Of course, if God does not seem real to you, your loneliness will be unabated. But try sharing your concerns, your joys, and your sorrows, and listen and expect a response from God. As He responds, your loneliness will disappear. Couples with children are always a bit lonely when one child fails to keep in touch. They may have four, and while they appreciate hearing from three, they miss the one who doesn't communicate. God's situation is on a vaster scale and friends of God will make their love and concern known to Him. In their circle of friends, they will put Him in the center.

Some people are no help to the lonely, for the lonely seek people who will listen. God is beset by people who share their troubles and concerns with Him, but never let God speak to them. God, too, seeks those who will listen. This may seem strange, and you may ask, "Why would God want to share his thoughts with me? I am so small, one of the billions like me, but there is only one of Him." The greatness of God is beyond our understanding. He cares and, in return, we can make certain that God is never lonely. Let us give Him thanks and praise daily, as becomes the children of God.

Recommended time of silence

As much as you need.

Break silence when ready and go with God.

****

FOR INFORMATION ABOUT COMING RETREATS AND RETREAT CENTERS

write:

The Cathedral of the Prince of Peace
Highlandville, Missouri 65669

or

phone:

(417) 587-3951

BIBLIOGRAPHY

Casteel, John L. *Renewal in Retreats.* New York: Association Press, 1959, 250 p.

Doherty, Catherine de Hueck. *Poustinia.* Notre Dame, Indiana: Ave Maria Press, 1974, 216 p.

Magee, Raymond J. *Call to Adventure.* Nashville: Abingdon, 1967, 169 p.

Merton, Thomas. *The Silent Life.* New York: Farrar, Straus, & Giroux, 1957, 178 p.

Picard, Max. *The World of Silence.* South Bend, Indiana: Gateway Editions, 1948, 231 p.

Prüter, Karl. *The People of God.* Scottsdale, Arizona: St. Willibrord's Press, 1974, 162 p.

Steere, Douglas V. *Time to Spare.* New York: Harper & Brothers, 1949, 187 p.

INDEX

ABOUT THE AUTHOR

Bishop Karl Prüter was born in 1920 in Poughkeepsie, New York. After completing high school there he did undergraduate work at Boston's Northeastern University, and then earned his master's degree in divinity at the Lutheran Theological Seminary in Philadelphia. After starting his ecclesiastical career as a congregational minister, he authored two books, the second of which, *Neo-Congregationalism*, was later revised to include a chapter relating the personal sojourn that brought him to the Old Catholic Movement.

In 1967 Prüter was consecrated bishop of Christ Catholic Church, and the church, under his leadership, has had significant influence on the entire Old Catholic Movement. He served as the presiding bishop of Christ Catholic Church from 1967 to June 1991, when he became suffragan bishop in order to have more time to devote to spiritual writing and to promoting the retreat movement. Throughout his work in the church, Bishop Prüter has conducted literally hundreds of retreats for both Protestant and Catholic groups.

Along with having written scores of religious pamphlets, the bishop has also authored eight books, among them *The Teachings of the Great Mystics, A History of the Old Catholic Church*, and *The Priest's Handbook*. He currently resides in Highlandville, Missouri, where he serves the Cathedral of the Prince of Peace, which is listed in the *Guinness Book of World Records* as the world's smallest cathedral, measuring 14-x-17 feet and seating 18 people.

56

www.ingramcontent.com/pod-product-compliance
Lightning Source LLC
Chambersburg PA
CBHW021349090426
42742CB00008B/792